# A Celebration Of Sisters

*Brownlow*

BROWNLOW PUBLISHING COMPANY, INC.

Copyright © 1996
Brownlow Publishing Company
6309 Airport Freeway
Fort Worth, Texas 76117

ISBN: 1-57051-129-2

Cover/Interior: *Koechel Peterson & Associates*

Printed in USA

# A Special Gift

To

.................................................................................

From

.................................................................................

Date

.................................................................................

# Ribbons of Love

A Celebration of Sisters

Christmas Wishes from the Heart

Gardens of Friendship

Happy Is the House That Shelters a Friend

In the Presence of Angels

Just for You: *A Celebration of Joy and Friendship*

Loving Thoughts for Tender Hearts

Mother: *Another Word for Love*

## For Carol & Holly Jo

Only sisters hear the echoes
of their mother's voice and preserve
the memories of home.

# A Love of Family

So much of what is best in us is bound up
in our love of family, that it remains the measure of
our stability because it measures our sense of loyalty.
All other pacts of love or fear derive from it
and are modeled upon it.

HANIEL LONG

# If I Had Known

If I had known what trouble you were bearing;

What griefs were in the silence of your face;

I would have been more gentle

and more caring, And tried to

give you gladness for a space.

MARY CAROLYN DAVIES

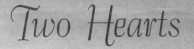

# Two Hearts

Two souls with but a single thought,
Two hearts that beat as one.

·◇·

VON MÜNCH BELLINGHAUSEN

*H*ome is a place
where the great are small,
and the small are great.

*O*ur Lord does not care so
much for the importance of our works as
for the love with which they are done.

••◇••

TERESA OF AVILA

# Sisters

The desire to be and have a sister is a primitive and profound one that may have everything or nothing to do with the family a woman is born to. It is a desire to know and be known by someone who shares blood and body, history and dreams, common ground and the unknown adventures of the future, darkest secrets and the glassiest beads of truth.

··◇··

ELIZABETH FISHEL

# The Energies of Love

Someday, after we have mastered the air, the winds, the tides and gravity, we will harness for God the energies of love. And then, for the second time in the history of the world, man will have discovered fire.

··◇··

PIERRE TEILHARD DE CHARDIN

A true sister is a friend who listens with her heart.

··◇··

ANONYMOUS

# I Tried

$\mathcal{M}$ake a rule, and pray to God to help you to keep it,

never, if possible, to lie down at night without being

able to say: "I have made one human being a little wiser,

or a little happier, or at least a little better this day."

❖

CHARLES KINGSLEY

*T*o love is to receive a glimpse of heaven.

•••◇•••

KAREN SUNDE

*N*o soul is desolate as long as there is a human
being for whom it can feel trust and reverence.

•••◇•••

GEORGE ELIOT

# Help Us, Lord

Help us, O Lord!
   with patient love to bear
Each other's faults,
   to suffer with true meekness.
Help us each other's joys
   and griefs to share,
But let us turn to
   Thee alone in weakness.

# A Blessing

Having some place to go is home.

Having someone to love is family.

Having both is a blessing.

•◇•

ANONYMOUS

Sisters and friends are God's life preservers.

# Best Friends

Often, in old age, they become each other's chosen and most happy companions. In addition to their shared memories of childhood and of their relationship to each other's children, they share memories of the same home, the same homemaking style, and the same small prejudices about housekeeping that carry the echoes of their mother's voice.

MARGARET MEAD

# Sweeter Every Day

*I*f I live by the human equivalents of grace, love,
forgiveness and faith with those who occupy space in my life,
thinking more of belonging than of owning, seeking to maintain
the relationship as a matter of supreme importance, those
relationships will never grow "stale," but sweeter every day.

···◇···

SANDRA W. HOOVER

# No Friend Like a Sister

For there is no friend like a sister,

In calm or stormy weather,

To cheer one on the tedious way,

To fetch one if one goes astray,

To lift one if one totters down,

To strengthen whilst one stands.

••◊••

CHRISTINA ROSSETTI

# We Need Each Other

We are born helpless. As soon as we
are fully conscious we discover loneliness.
We need others physically, emotionally,
intellectually; we need them
if we are to know anything,
even ourselves.

C. S. LEWIS

# The Gift of Encouragement

*Therefore encourage one another and build each other up, just as in fact you are doing.*

···◇···

1 THESSALONIANS 5:11

# A Blessing for the Home

The crown of the home is godliness;

The beauty of the home is order;

The glory of the home is hospitality;

The blessing of the home is contentment.

•··◇··•

HENRY VAN DYKE

The best cure for worry, depression, melancholy,

brooding, is to go deliberately forth and try to lift with

one's sympathy the gloom of somebody else.

•··◇··•

ARNOLD BENNETT

*A* family will hold together across the years if each member refrains from pointing the accusing finger.

••◇••

JOHN MILLER

*I* wonder why it is that we are not all kinder to each other than we are. How much the world needs it! How easily it is done.

••◇••

HENRY DRUMMOND

# In Our Hands

Parents can only give good advice or put them on the right paths, but the final forming of a person's character lies in their own hands.

ANNE FRANK

# The Way of Love

The way to love someone is to lightly run your
finger over that person's soul until you find a crack,
and then gently pour your love into that crack.

❖

KEITH MILLER

*It is hard to believe that anything is
worthwhile, unless...what is infinitely precious
to us is precious alike to another mind.*

❖

GEORGE ELIOT

# A Friend

She had come to be a friend and companion such as few possessed—intelligent, well-informed, useful, gentle, knowing all the ways of the family, interested in all its concerns, and peculiarly interested in Emma, in every pleasure, every scheme of hers; one to whom Emma could speak every thought as it arose, and who had such an affection for her as could never find fault.

JANE AUSTEN

# Sunshine Faces

How sweet and gaily
>    The fleet moments glide,
When warmed by the sunshine
>    Of faces we love!

# Love Alone

*L*ove alone is capable of uniting living beings
in such a way as to complete and
fulfill them, for it alone takes them
and joins them by what is
deepest in themselves.

··◇··

PIERRE TEILHARD DE CHARDIN

*I* like not only to be loved,

but to be told I am loved.

·◇·

GEORGE ELIOT

*F*amily jokes, though rightly

cursed by strangers, are the bond that

keeps most families alive.

·◇·

STELLA BENSON

# A Family

Call it a clan, call it a network,
call it a tribe, call it a family. Whatever
you call it, whoever you are, you need one.

❖

JANE HOWARD

A kindhearted woman gains respect.

❖

PROVERBS 11:16

# A Charming Companion

*I*t is always good to know,

if only in passing,

a charming human being;

it refreshes our lives

like flowers and woods

and clear brooks.

⬧

GEORGE ELIOT

# Her Part Was Deeds

There was little of patronizing benevolence about her; her earnest kindness, her active goodness, darting at once to the truth and right of things, touched hearts. She never indulged in verbal sentimentalism. Her part in the world was deeds.

••◇••

DINAH MARIA MULOCK

# To Really Live

You will find, as you look back upon your life, that

the moments when you have really lived are the moments

when you have done things in the spirit of love.

HENRY DRUMMOND

$\mathcal{T}$here can be no situation in life
in which the conversation of my dear sister
will not administer some comfort to me.

❖

LADY MARY WORTLEY MONTAGU

# Cheerful Hearts

A happy woman is one who has no cares at all; a cheerful woman is one who has cares but doesn't let them get her down.

◆

BEVERLY SILLS

# My Sister

My sister! With that thrilling word
　　　Let thoughts unnumbered wildly spring!
What echoes in my heart are stirred,
　　　While thus I touch the trembling string.

◆

MARGARET DAVIDSON

# The One Place

Home is the one place in all this world where hearts are sure of each other. It is the place of confidence. It is the place where we tear off that mask of guarded and suspicious coldness which the world forces us to wear in self-defense, and where we pour out the unreserved communications of full and confiding hearts. It is the spot where expressions of tenderness gush out without any sensation of awkwardness and without any dread of ridicule.

FREDERICK W. ROBERTSON

# At Home

Strength of character may be acquired at work,
but beauty of character is learned at home.
There the affections are trained. There the gentle
life reaches us, the true heaven life.

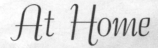

HENRY DRUMMOND

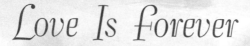

# Love Is Forever

Time flies,

Suns rise

And shadows fall.

Let time go by.

Love is forever over all.

ANONYMOUS

# I Wish You Peace

**M**ay your home be filled with peace,

And your heart with hopeful cheer,

May your happiness increase

With each bright succeeding year.

❖

H. M. BURNSIDE

*T*raveling in the company
of those we love is home in motion.

◆

LEIGH HUNT

*A* new command I give you:
Love one another. As I have loved you,
so you must love one another.

◆

JOHN 13:34

# Two Sisters

As Jesus and his disciples were on their way, he came to a village where a woman named Martha opened her home to him. She had a sister called Mary, who sat at the Lord's feet listening to what he said. But Martha was distracted by all the preparations that had to be made. She came to him and asked, "Lord, don't you care that my sister has left me to do the work by myself? Tell her to help me!"

"Martha, Martha," the Lord answered, "you are worried and upset about many things, but only one thing is needed. Mary has chosen what is better, and it will not be taken away from her."

••◇••

Luke 10:38–42

# The Pursuit of Happiness

Half of the world is on the wrong scent in the pursuit of happiness. They think it consists in having and getting, and in being served by others. It consists in giving and in serving others.

HENRY DRUMMOND

*L*oving relationships are a family's best
protection against the challenges of the world.

B. WIEBE

*T*here's something so beautiful in coming on one's
very own inmost thoughts in another. In one way
it's one of the greatest pleasures one has.

OLIVE SCHREINER

# A Celebration of Sisters

Growing up, sisters really do share so much. They share
the same memories, the same household chores,
the same holiday traditions, the same relatives,
the same clothes, and often the same room.

And while time and age gives to each sister some
new experiences, even these get "shared" as one story after
another comes tumbling out when they get together.

But ultimately, sisters share more than just time and
space together; they share their hearts.

# The Dignity of Parenthood

Be ever ready to listen to the smallest of little mysteries,

knowing that nothing to childhood is too trivial for the

notice, too foolish for the sympathy, of those on whom the

Father of all has bestowed the dignity of parenthood.

DINAH MARIA MULOCK

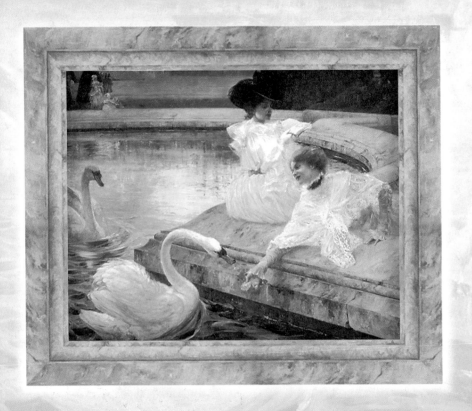

*T*he woman who creates and sustains a home and under whose hands children grow up to be strong and pure men and women is a creator second only to God.

‥◇‥

HELEN MARIA FISKE HUNT JACKSON

*L*abor and trouble one can always get through alone,
but it takes two to be glad.

⬦

HENRIK IBSEN

*T*he great tragedy of life is not that men perish,
but that they cease to love.

⬦

W. SOMERSET MAUGHAM

$L$ove is the only thing that
we can carry with us when we go,
and it makes the end so easy.

••◇••

LOUISA MAY ALCOTT

# Home of
# the Happy

Happy are the families
where the government of
parents is the reign of affection,
and obedience of the children
is the submission of love.

BACON

Only when the heart loves can the intellect do great work.

••◇••

N. D. HILLIS

Dear children, let us not love with words or
tongue but with actions and in truth.

••◇••

1 JOHN 3:18

Home is not where you live but where they understand you.

••◇••

CHRISTIAN MORGENSTERN

# The Family

The family—that dear octopus from
whose tentacles we never quite escape, nor,
in our inmost hearts, ever quite wish to.

··◇··

DODIE SMITH

*I*t is not enough to love those who are near
and dear to us. We must show them that we do so.

•••◊•••

LORD AVEBURY

*K*indness is a golden chain by which society
is bound together.

•••◊•••

GOETHE

# Home

## A world of care without,
A world of strife shut out,
A world of love shut in.

◦◇◦

DORA GREENWELL

$B$etter do a good deed near at
home than go far away to burn incense.

⋯◇⋯

CHINESE PROVERB

$W$hoever is happy will make others happy too.

⋯◇⋯

ANNE FRANK

$A$mong God's best gifts to us
Are the people who love us.

*L*ove understands love; it needs no talk.

••◇••

FRANCES RIDLEY HAVERGAL

*H*e who is filled with love is filled
with God Himself.

••◇••

AUGUSTINE

*I*f things go well with the family,
life is worth living; when the family falters,
life falls apart.

••◇••

MICHAEL NOVAK

*L*ove and faithfulness meet together;

righteousness and peace kiss each other.

••◇••

PSALM 85:10

*G*rief can take care of itself; but to get the full value of joy

you must have somebody to divide it with.

••◇••

MARK TWAIN

*A* happy family is but an earlier heaven.

••◇••

SIR JOHN BOWRING

# Too Late

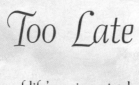

One of life's major mistakes
is being the last member of
the family to get the flu—
after all the sympathy
has run out.

# families

**W**hat families have in common
the world around is that they are the place
where people learn who they are
and how to be that way.

··◇··

JEAN ILLSLEY CLARKE

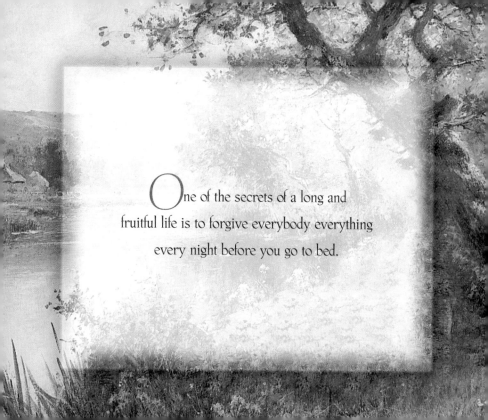

One of the secrets of a long and fruitful life is to forgive everybody everything every night before you go to bed.

*T*o love anyone is nothing else than
to wish that person good.

THOMAS AQUINAS

*M*y sister! my sweet sister! if a name
Dearer and purer were, it should be thine.

LORD BYRON

*I* believe in hard work. It keeps the wrinkles out of the mind
and the spirit. It helps to keep a woman young.

HELENA RUBINSTEIN

*D*o unto others as though you were the others.

*H*ome: where each lives
for the other and all live for God.

*S*peak your kind words soon, for you never
know how soon it will be too late.

# Beauty for the Day

*I* still find each day too short for all the thoughts
I want to think, all the walks I want to take, all the
books I want to read, and all the friends I want to see.
The longer I live, the more my mind dwells upon
the beauty and wonder of the world.

JOHN BURROUGHS

# Home

Home is where affections bind
    Gentle hearts in union,
Where voices all are kind,
    Together holding sweet communion.

# Hearts at Home

**W**here we love is home,
Home that our feet may leave,
but not our hearts.

OLIVER WENDELL HOLMES

**A** kind word is never lost. It keeps going on,
from one person to another, until it
comes back to you again.

# Two Are Better

Two are better than one,

because they have a good

return for their work:

If one falls down,

his friend can help him up.

ECCLESIASTES 4:9, 10

$U$nless the LORD builds the house,

its builders labor in vain.

•••◇•••

PSALM 127:1

$S$isterhood is powerful.

•••◇•••

ROBIN MORGAN

# Remember the Kitchen

*N*ostalgia is remembering the
pleasures of our old kitchen when we were kids,
without remembering how long it took
to wash the dishes.